W9-AFK-586

ALCOHOL

BY LISA J. AMSTUTZ

CONTENT CONSULTANT
EUN-YOUNG MUN
PROFESSOR, DEPARTMENT OF HEALTH BEHAVIOR AND HEALTH SYSTEMS
UNIVERSITY OF NORTH TEXAS HEALTH SCIENCE CENTER

An Imprint of Abdo Publishing | abdopublishing.com

ABDOPUBLISHING.COM

Published by Abdo Publishing, a division of ABDO, PO Box 398166, Minneapolis, Minnesota 55439.
Copyright © 2019 by Abdo Consulting Group, Inc. International copyrights reserved in all countries.
No part of this book may be reproduced in any form without written permission from the publisher.
Essential Library™ is a trademark and logo of Abdo Publishing.

Printed in the United States of America, North Mankato, Minnesota
042018
092018

 THIS BOOK CONTAINS
RECYCLED MATERIALS

Cover Photo: Shutterstock Images
Interior Photos: Artem Furman/Shutterstock Images, 5; Yacob Chuk/iStockphoto, 7; Andrew
Matthews/Press Association/PA Wire URN:34302875/AP Images, 10–11; Elena Elisseeva Stock
Connection Worldwide/Newscom, 15; Shutterstock Images, 17 (top), 17 (middle), 17 (bottom),
22–23, 46–47, 57, 58; Damian Dovarganes/AP Images, 18; Kelvin Murray/Taxi/Getty Images, 21;
José Pazos Fabián/Notimex/Newscom, 25; Falkensteinfoto/Alamy, 28; Christina Kennedy/Alamy,
34; BSIP/Newscom, 36–37; Tom Wang/Shutterstock Images, 40; iStockphoto, 48–49, 61, 65, 79, 96;
Medicimage/Universal Images Group North America LLC/Alamy, 52–53; Monkey Business Images/
Shutterstock Images, 66–67; J. Kyle Keener/Pharos-Tribune/AP Images, 70–71; Tom Williams/CQ Roll
Call/AP Images, 74; F. Gorgun/iStockphoto, 76; Rick Bowmer/AP Images, 81; Kyndell Harkness/Star
Tribune/AP Images, 82; Jim Lambert/Alamy, 84–85; Richard Levine/Alamy, 87; wonderlandstock/
Alamy, 91; Michael Flippo/Alamy, 93; Steve Debenport/iStockphoto, 99

Editor: Alyssa Krekelberg
Series Designer: Laura Polzin

Library of Congress Control Number: 2017961348

Publisher's Cataloging-in-Publication Data

Names: Amstutz, Lisa J., author.
Title: Alcohol / by Lisa J. Amstutz.
Description: Minneapolis, Minnesota : Abdo Publishing, 2019. | Series: Drugs in real life
    | Includes online resources and index.
Identifiers: ISBN 9781532114120 (lib.bdg.) | ISBN 9781532153952 (ebook)
Subjects: LCSH: Alcoholics--Juvenile literature. | Alcoholism--United States--Juvenile literature.
    | Drug addicts--Alcohol use--Juvenile literature. | Drug control--United States--
    Juvenile literature.
Classification: DDC 362.292--dc23

CONTENTS

A SERIOUS PROBLEM

Brianna took her first sip of wine at a friend's house in seventh grade. "We only took a little and the minute it hit my lips, I knew I loved drinking. I loved how it made me feel," she said.[1] It would be the first of countless drinks she consumed over the next decade. Being drunk made Brianna feel more fun and exciting, and she believed that it helped her cope with her severe social anxiety.

Throughout high school and college, Brianna's drinking was limited by her parents, who were especially protective because of their family history of alcohol abuse. She got good grades and held down a job. However, when she finished college, Brianna

moved out of her parents' house and started to drink in earnest. Her job as a waitress and bartender provided her with free drinks, and she was soon partying almost every night. If her friends didn't want to join her, she felt sad and alone. When Brianna was 22, she began having nightly blackouts—periods of time that she could not remember. Her life became more dangerous as she found herself climbing onto rooftops, hitchhiking, swimming in unsafe rivers, and going home with strangers. "I did these things because I had stopped caring about myself and I simultaneously needed to push the limits," Brianna said. "I had this idea that I would be a 'beautiful disaster.'"[2]

The term *alcohol* comes from an Arabic word, *al-kuhul,* meaning "kohl." Kohl is a powder used in certain traditional cultures as a cosmetic.[3]

By age 24, Brianna had hit rock bottom. She had lost her family and friends, her job, her car, her boyfriend, and even her dog. Still, she could not stop drinking. Finally, she had a moment of clarity at a music festival. She had no money for alcohol and, without it, she felt as though she could not join in with the fun going on around her. Her pain and sadness made her realize she needed help.

Brianna entered an inpatient treatment center in 2014 and began the process of recovery. As of 2017, she remained sober and in control of her life. She built new, healthy relationships and repaired her ties with her family. After Brianna became sober,

Families of people with alcohol addictions sometimes don't understand why their loved ones can't stop drinking.

she got a job helping other women recover from their own

addictions at the same treatment center that helped her.

ALCOHOL USE AND MISUSE

Alcohol has long been part of celebrations, traditions, and

religious ceremonies around the world. Used in moderation,

it may have some health benefits and make some people feel

relaxed, uninhibited, and confident. Drinking alcohol is legal

for adults of a certain age and is common in the United States.

It's so common that people tend to underestimate its dangers.

Some chemicals found in alcohol are toxic. While most people's

bodies can tolerate small amounts of these toxins, heavy use

can damage a person's brain, liver, and heart. The toxins can

also cause cancer and even result in severe alcohol poisoning

or death. Heavy alcohol consumption can lead to mental

Alcohol is a general term used to describe a drink made from grains, fruits, or vegetables. Yeasts break down sugars in these foods into a chemical called ethyl alcohol, or ethanol. Ethanol is also used in manufacturing processes and as a gasoline additive.

LEGAL VS. ILLEGAL DRUGS

Some drugs in the United States are legal, while others are not. For example, alcohol is legal for people age 21 and older. Caffeine is found in many common beverages such as soft drinks and coffee and is available for anyone to consume. Over-the-counter medications and drugs prescribed for medical conditions are also legal when patients use them as intended. However, some people abuse these drugs, which include tranquilizers, painkillers, sedatives, and amphetamines.

Medical marijuana use is legal in some states, and a few states permit the recreational use of this drug as well. Other drugs, such as heroin, cocaine, LSD, and methamphetamine, are illegal in every state.

illnesses such as anxiety and depression. This abuse can lead to other dangers as well, such as unwanted sexual activity, drowning, vehicle accidents, and violence. Approximately 88,000 deaths per year in the United States can be attributed to excessive drinking.[4]

The majority of American adults consume at least some alcohol. The 2015 National Survey on Drug Use and Health found that 86.4 percent of people aged 18 and up have had a drink of alcohol. Of this percentage, 70.1 percent had a drink in the past year and 56.0 percent in the past month.[5]

Many people engage only in social drinking, which is drinking on special occasions or having an occasional drink with friends after work or with dinner. Binge drinking and heavy alcohol use are less common, but these types of alcohol use cause a disproportionate amount of health and social problems. Binge drinking happens when people consume large amounts of alcohol very quickly. Heavy alcohol use is often defined as binge drinking on five or more days per month. It's also defined as more than 4 drinks on any day or 14 drinks per week for men, and more than 3 drinks on any day or 7 per week for women. In a 2015 survey, 26.9 percent of people 18 and older reported at least one binge drinking episode in the past month, and 7 percent reported heavy alcohol use.[6]

When people's drinking causes them distress or harms their physical, mental, or emotional health, a doctor may diagnose them with a medical condition known as alcohol use disorder (AUD). According to the American Psychiatric Association, AUD is a pattern of alcohol use that causes significant problems for the user, as shown by two or more negative behavioral

THE CAGE QUESTIONNAIRE

In 1970, Dr. John Ewing, who is the founding director for Bowles Centre for Alcohol Studies, developed a questionnaire to help people determine whether they were dependent on alcohol. It's known as the CAGE questionnaire. The acronym CAGE stands for Cut down, Annoyed, Guilty, and Eye opener. Each response is scored with either a zero or one. A score of two or higher is considered a possible sign of AUD. Questions include: "Have you ever felt you should cut down on your drinking?", "Have people annoyed you by criticizing your drinking?", "Have you ever felt bad or guilty about your drinking?", and "Have you ever had a drink first thing in the morning to steady your nerves or to get rid of a hangover?"[7]

People who have AUD struggle to moderate their alcohol intake.

patterns within the period of one year. These behaviors include
using alcohol despite experiencing negative consequences such
as physical, legal, or social problems or difficulty performing
well at work, school, or home. The disorder is diagnosed as mild,
moderate, or severe depending on how many of these criteria
are met.

AUD can take the form of a physical or mental addiction. People with AUD feel a strong craving, or need, to drink in order to deal with uncomfortable emotions or physical withdrawal symptoms. They often feel they need a drink—or many drinks— just to get through the day. The term *alcoholic* is often used to refer to someone with this type of disorder.

People with AUD often find themselves drinking more than they intended, or needing increasing amounts of alcohol to achieve the same feeling of intoxication. The latter is known as tolerance. People with AUD may try unsuccessfully to quit drinking despite the problems their drinking causes. People with AUD spend considerable amounts of time obtaining alcohol, drinking it, and recovering from its effects. Once people have developed this condition, it is very difficult for them to quit drinking. When they try to stop, they often experience painful withdrawal symptoms.

Even after years of sobriety, a single drink can send a person recovering from AUD back into full-blown addiction. AUD is considered a chronic disease. People, places, things, or certain times of day associated with alcohol can act as triggers for drinking, especially during the first six months of recovery. Many people with AUD relapse at some point. Ongoing therapy can help patients reduce the likelihood of this happening.

WHAT IS TOLERANCE?

People who regularly drink large amounts of alcohol can build up a tolerance to it. This means that they need to drink increasing amounts to achieve the same effect. This can be dangerous, as drinking large quantities of alcohol can damage the brain and other organs. Tolerance can have several different causes. It can result from genetics. Studies have also found that when people do tasks while intoxicated, they develop tolerance faster. This is known as learned tolerance.

However, the craving for alcohol may never completely disappear, and some people may require lifelong treatment to maintain their sobriety. In 2015, 2.5 percent of people aged 12 to 17 and 6.2 percent of adults in the United States were affected by AUD.[8]

Alcohol can be an important part of cultural and religious life when used appropriately by adults. However, it poses serious risks when it is abused—especially for young people. Alcohol abuse can cause severe physical and psychological effects. It can also lead to dangerous situations such as drunk driving. However, recovery from alcohol abuse is possible with the right type of treatment.

DISEASE OR LACK OF WILLPOWER?

For centuries, people thought AUD was a moral failing or character flaw. They assumed the addicted person had a lack of self-control or willpower. However, scientists have come to understand addiction as a brain disease. US surgeon general Vivek H. Murthy wrote in his 2016 Report on Alcohol, Drugs, and Health:

For far too long, too many in our country have viewed addiction as a moral failing. This unfortunate stigma has created an added burden of shame that has made people with substance use disorders less likely to come forward and seek help. It has also made it more challenging to marshal the necessary investments in prevention and treatment. We must help everyone see that addiction is not a character flaw—it is a chronic illness that we must approach with the same skill and compassion with which we approach heart disease, diabetes, and cancer.[9]

CHAPTER TWO

HOW ALCOHOL IS MADE

Alcoholic drinks come in many different forms and strengths. They can be grouped into three main types: beers, wines, and spirits. The process for making each of these is somewhat different.

Beer is made from hops, water, some kind of malted grain, and microorganisms known as yeasts. Hops are cone-shaped flowers from the hop plant, a climbing vine. They add flavor and aroma, and they help preserve the beer. The most commonly used grain is barley, but wheat, corn, rice, oats, and rye can be used as well. Beer typically contains approximately 5 percent alcohol.[1] Its alcohol content is lower than that of many other

Stainless steel vats are frequently used by alcohol manufacturers during the fermentation process.

▶

alcoholic drinks, so people have to drink more of it to feel its effects.

Wine is an alcoholic beverage made from various types of fruit—most commonly grapes—and yeast. To make wine, the fruit is first crushed and strained. Natural yeasts in the air cause the fruit to ferment, but winemakers often add their own yeast cultures as well to ensure consistency. After it ferments for 10 to 30 days, or even longer in some cases, the wine is filtered and sealed into bottles. The alcohol content of a standard glass of wine is around 12 percent.[2]

Distilled spirits, also known as hard liquor or hard alcohol, are made by combining yeast with grains, fruits, or vegetables. These beverages are made by distilling a fermented drink to increase its alcohol content to a higher level than would naturally occur. A standard serving of distilled spirits is 40 percent alcohol.[3] However, many types of distilled liquors have much higher alcohol content, even

A STANDARD DRINK[4]

12 ounces (350 mL) of beer

APPROXIMATELY
5 PERCENT ALCOHOL

5 ounces (150 mL) of wine

APPROXIMATELY
12 PERCENT ALCOHOL

1.5 ounces (44 mL) of distilled spirits

APPROXIMATELY
40 PERCENT ALCOHOL

Each of these drinks is considered one standard drink of alcohol.

Students at California State Polytechnic University can take courses on how to brew beer.

approaching 100 percent. Because of their high alcohol content, it takes only a small amount of distilled spirits for a drinker to become intoxicated.

THE SCIENCE OF FERMENTATION

Alcohol is produced by a process called fermentation. Yeasts are typically added to mashed grain or fruit and allowed to multiply. These microorganisms feed on sugars such as glucose, sucrose, and fructose in the mash and release energy in the form of adenosine triphosphate. Yeasts use this energy to grow and reproduce. The yeast creates ethanol and carbon dioxide as by-products of this multistep process. The ethanol makes the drink alcoholic, and the carbon dioxide makes the finished product taste fizzy.

The word *fermentation* comes from a Latin word, *fervere*, which means "to boil." This is because the bubbles formed in fermenting juices make the juices look as if they are boiling.

When ancient peoples made alcoholic beverages, the alcohol content and flavor were inconsistent. Today, the beverage industry has the process of fermentation down to a science. For example, early wine producers trampled their grapes with their feet and then let the mash stand in open containers, introducing yeast into the process. Modern winemakers heat the mash to kill undesirable microorganisms and then add carefully selected yeasts to ensure a consistent product. The process usually takes place in large, closed stainless steel vats that are carefully temperature controlled.

Yeast fermentation also takes place when bread is baked. The carbon dioxide bubbles released cause the bread to rise. A tiny bit of alcohol is produced in this process, but because the dough is not allowed to ferment very long, this amount is minimal.

THE DISTILLATION PROCESS

Nature limits the alcohol content of fermented drinks when traditional varieties of yeast are used. It cannot rise above 18 percent because at that point, the alcohol kills off the yeast and fermentation stops.[5] However, people long ago figured out ways to raise the alcohol content to a much higher level through a process known as distillation.

This process works because ethanol and water boil at different temperatures. Ethanol has a boiling point of 173.3 degrees Fahrenheit (78.5°C). Water has a boiling point of 212 degrees Fahrenheit (100°C). Heating a liquid containing ethanol to a temperature between these boiling points causes the ethanol to boil off, but not the water. The ethanol steam is captured and cooled to condense it back into a liquid, which now has a much higher concentration of ethanol than before. The process can be repeated several times to condense the alcohol even further.

Grapes are the most commonly used raw material for making distilled spirits—they are fermented and distilled into brandy. Other fruits, such as apples and peaches, are also used for making brandy. Vegetables such as sugarcane,

DISTILLING TOOLS

Distillation requires a fairly basic three-part apparatus commonly known as a still. A pot or boiler holds and heats the mash, which is grains, fruits, or vegetables that have been mashed. The mash ferments, giving off alcohol, which is evaporated by the heat. A condenser cools the steam, turning it back into a liquid, and a receiver collects the condensed product, which is known as the distillate. Because alcohol evaporates at a lower temperature than water, the distillate has a much higher concentration of alcohol than the original mixture did. There are many different types of stills, but all contain these elements.

Customers can purchase and drink liquor made on-site at some distilleries.

sugar beets, and the *Agave tequilana* cactus can be made into spirits as well. Corn, rye, rice, barley, wheat, and potatoes can be distilled into whiskey and other liquors.

Certain types of spirits, such as rum, brandy, and whiskey, must be aged after they are distilled. They are usually aged in wooden casks made of white oak. The wood allows air to reach the liquid and adds flavor. The aging period for brandy is usually 3 to 5 years but can be up to 40 years or more. Rum and whiskey are aged for 2 to 3 years.[6]

ALCOHOL AND CULTURE

People have been producing alcohol for at least 9,000 years. It played important roles in religious celebrations in many ancient cultures. Alcoholic drinks also served as an important source of calories, allowing farmers to store foods in a form that would not quickly spoil, for times when food was scarce. Most of these cultures developed societal norms, or rules, for the use of alcohol. These norms helped prevent people from overindulging in alcohol. The drinks they made also had relatively low alcohol content, making it difficult to drink enough to become drunk.

In 2004, at a site called Jiahu in China, archaeologists discovered broken pieces of ancient pots. The fragments

contained residue of drinks made with grapes and hawthorn wine, honey mead, and rice beer. The archaeologists dated the shards to approximately 7000 BCE. Pots from 5400 to 5000 BCE containing beer and wine residue have also been found in Iran. Around this time, early farmers in the Middle East began growing grains to make beer and bread. The beer had a low alcohol content, but it contained valuable nutrients and may have been safer to drink than water, which was often contaminated due to poor sanitation. The antiseptic properties of alcohol would have killed off most harmful organisms.

The ancient Greeks used wine, usually mixed with water, to make their water safe for drinking. It was also used as a source of calories, as medicine, and as a religious symbol. Wine played an important role in Greek culture. However, the Greeks frowned on drunkenness. They thought it represented bad citizenship and ungentlemanly conduct. The exception to this belief occurred during the annual festival celebrating Dionysus, who was the Greek god of wine. During this festival, revelers could drink without judgment.

Alcohol played an important role in northern European cultures as well. Some of these cultures had fewer social rules about drunkenness. For instance, the Celts drank beer daily and celebrated many holidays by feasting and drinking ale.

Some early cultures in Central and South America developed different forms of alcohol. These included chicha, a fermented drink made primarily from corn, and pulque, a thick drink made from the juice of the maguey cactus. Pulque is still produced in rural parts of Mexico today.

MEDICAL USES AND CONNECTIONS TO RELIGION

Along with its cultural and caloric value, alcohol's antiseptic and anesthetic properties made it valuable for medical use in ancient times. Alcohol can kill microorganisms, including disease-causing bacteria. The Greeks used wine mixed with clean water and vinegar to clean wounds. They also used alcohol to help numb pain before anesthetics were available. In the Middle East,

Pulque is a well-known Mexican beverage.

One ancient Sumerian prescription for treating wounds read, "Pound together fur-turpentine, pine-turpentine, tamarisk, daisy, flour of inninnu(;) strain; mix in milk and beer in a small copper pan; spread on skin; bind on him, and he shall recover."[1]

the ancient Sumerians mixed beer with other substances to clean wounds. The Nubians of northeastern Africa seem to have taken this practice one step further and brewed special medicinal beers containing a natural antibiotic.

Throughout history, many cultures have associated alcohol with religious ceremonies. For example, beginning around 2040 BCE, the Egyptians celebrated the annual Tekh Festival, or Feast of Drunkenness. Other ancient Egyptian festivals also included large quantities of beer. People also buried beer with the dead for their use in the afterlife and offered it to their gods in temples.

In South Africa, the Zulu goddess Mbaba Mwana Waresa was credited with inventing beer. The Gauls of western Europe worshipped Sucellus, the Celtic god of agriculture and wine. Early Christians used wine in their Communion ceremonies, and many groups of Christians continue this practice today.

ALCOHOL GETS STRONGER

By 800 BCE, the Chinese had figured out how to distill rice beer into a stronger drink. The Arabs, Greeks, and Romans also started producing distilled spirits around this time. Spain, France, and other European cultures may have also distilled drinks, but they do not seem to have become common anywhere until 700–800 CE. Early distilled spirits included grape brandy, which was made from wine, and distilled mead, which was made from honey.

Before distillation was invented, the low alcohol content of most drinks made it difficult for anyone to drink enough in a short time to get seriously intoxicated. With new distillation technology, alcohol content in drinks increased. Drunkenness became more of a problem. The availability of cheap distilled spirits turned alcohol into a drug of choice in many cultures. For instance, when gin made its appearance in England in the 1700s, the number of incidents of public drunkenness, violence, and rioting rose sharply. It caused serious problems for individuals, families, and society as a whole.

CHANGING CULTURAL VIEWS IN THE UNITED STATES

European settlers brought alcohol with them when they settled in North America. Most drank large amounts of beer, hard cider, wine, and whiskey. A few religious groups disapproved of drinking entirely, and others approved of drinking only in moderation. For example, the strict Pilgrim sect called alcohol the "Good Creature of God," and even their children drank it regularly.[2] But they considered drunkenness sinful. However,

as a whole, the colonists didn't view alcohol consumption as a problem.

Then, in the early 1800s, a shift occurred. Alcohol consumption began to rise as distilled spirits became more available and affordable in the United States. Most drinking had previously taken place in a family setting, but now more men began spending drunken nights at the saloon. Many people in the United States began to see heavy alcohol consumption as dangerous. At the same time, a religious revival swept through the country. A new temperance movement arose, aimed at fighting heavy alcohol consumption. Between the 1820s and 1920s, its supporters lobbied for a minimum drinking age and stronger laws regarding drinking. Supporters also tried to stop students from drinking on college campuses. They published many poems, books, plays, and other items with strong moralistic messages aimed at preventing people from drinking. One popular story, written in 1854, was called *Ten Nights in a Barroom and What I Saw There*. In the story, a man's daughter is killed when she comes to a bar to beg her father to come home and stop drinking. After more deaths occur, the townspeople pass laws against drinking and empty out the saloon.

PROHIBITION

The temperance movement peaked in the United States with the passing of the Eighteenth Amendment to the Constitution in

1919. The amendment prohibited people from making, selling, and transporting alcohol. The passage of this amendment marked the beginning of a period known as Prohibition.

Although its goal was to prevent crime, poverty, and other social problems associated with alcohol—and by extension improve the country's economy—the law resulted in a whole new set of issues. Illegal bars sprouted up everywhere. Some people turned to homemade drinks such as moonshine. These beverages were not always safe. A bad batch of liquor could cause blindness, paralysis, and even death. During Prohibition, approximately 1,000 people died every year from drinking tainted liquor.[3] Organized crime groups soon controlled much of the illegal alcohol trade.

AFRICAN AMERICANS AND ALCOHOL

The history of African Americans and alcohol in the United States is intertwined with the history of slavery. Enslaved people's access to alcohol was often tightly controlled by slaveholders. Alcohol was only allowed on holidays. Even free African Americans could not easily purchase alcohol during this period. Church-based temperance societies formed during the early 1800s and continued to grow after emancipation. When Prohibition came along, some African Americans saw it as an attempt to control them, while others, particularly clergy, supported it. After Prohibition ended, rates of alcohol use among African Americans remained slightly lower than those of society at large, and that trend continued into 2017.

People found creative ways to get around the laws. Pharmacists were allowed to dispense whiskey for medicinal purposes, so enterprising bootleggers set up their own pharmacies. Churches and synagogues were allowed to purchase wine for use in religious ceremonies, so suddenly many people started calling themselves rabbis or priests. Stores also sold kits for home winemaking.

The law was a failure in another sense: it did not help the economy as its promoters hoped. On the contrary, jobs were lost in the entertainment and restaurant industries, which relied heavily on liquor sales. States lost a significant source of tax revenue, as liquor had been heavily taxed before Prohibition. The state of New York, for example, lost 75 percent of its state tax revenue. The federal government lost billions in tax revenues, and it spent a total of $300 million to enforce the Prohibition laws.[4]

By the 1930s, a majority of people felt that repealing Prohibition was the most sensible thing to do. At this time, the United States was in the Great Depression. The Great Depression

WHAT IS MOONSHINE?

During Prohibition, many people turned to moonshine, which was illegal alcohol made in secret. Whiskey or rum was often produced in hidden backyard stills. Their owners visited them late at night—hence the term moonshine. Most moonshine produced in the United States was made from corn and was not aged, so it had a stronger flavor and often higher alcohol content than commercially produced versions.

began in 1929 and ended in 1939. During this period, the economy struggled and millions of people lost their jobs. Some people believed repealing Prohibition would provide jobs and tax money to help fund social programs. In 1933, under the leadership of President Franklin D. Roosevelt, Congress passed the Twenty-First Amendment, which repealed the Eighteenth Amendment. "What America needs now is a drink," Roosevelt is said to have quipped.[5] The United States' experiment in Prohibition had come to an end.

BOOTLEGGERS DURING PROHIBITION

People who transported and sold illegal alcohol were called bootleggers. During Prohibition, bootleggers smuggled foreign liquor into the United States from Mexico and Canada. Alcohol was also smuggled into the United States from foreign ships that docked along the coast. At a favorite meeting point near Atlantic City, New Jersey, rum-running ships met up with high-powered boats that could outrun the US Coast Guard. They transferred their goods to these boats, which then delivered the goods to shore.

A NEW PERSPECTIVE

In the 1700s and 1800s, few treatment options for AUD were available. But as society grew more aware and disapproving of the effects of excessive alcohol use, that gradually began to change. Some doctors started to see AUD as a medical condition, not simply as a character flaw. A few physicians and hospitals began offering treatment for AUD. By the early 1900s, AUD was seen by some physicians as a psychological problem.

Individuals with substance use disorders were sent to state mental hospitals or penal colonies along with mentally ill patients. Unfortunately, many of these institutions abused their patients, subjecting them to painful and ineffective treatments.

As time went on, more and better treatment clinics sprouted up. In 1935, Alcoholics Anonymous (AA) was founded. This group offers anonymous support from peers who struggle with alcohol addiction. Today, numerous other self-help organizations provide support for people with AUD and their families. Additionally, a number of evidence-based behavioral and pharmaceutical treatment options exist.

UNINTENDED EFFECTS OF PROHIBITION

In 1932, businessman John D. Rockefeller wrote to the *New York Times* regarding Prohibition. His letter showed some of the law's unintended effects:

> When the Eighteenth Amendment was passed I earnestly hoped . . . that it would be generally supported by public opinion and thus the day be hastened when the value to society of men with minds and bodies free from the undermining effects of alcohol would be generally realized. That this has not been the result . . . I have slowly and reluctantly come to believe.[6]

TRENDS TODAY

Overall, alcohol consumption generally rose during the last half of the 1900s, probably due to rising incomes, inexpensive

products, and heavy marketing by alcohol producers. In the United States, alcohol consumption increased by more than 50 percent after Prohibition and increased until the early 1980s, when it peaked.[7] The average annual US consumption of pure ethanol per person was 2.3 gallons (8.7 L) in 2012.[8]

Some cultures and religions continue to frown on drinking alcohol. For example, teachings of the Church of Jesus Christ of Latter-day Saints forbid alcohol use. Alcohol is also forbidden in the Islamic faith. Many people from Chinese, Italian, and Jewish cultures drink in moderation but do not look favorably upon getting drunk. As a result, these groups tend to have low rates of AUD. By contrast, the French have a much more tolerant attitude toward drunkenness and have much higher rates of alcohol-related illness and death.

CHAPTER FOUR

EFFECTS ON THE BRAIN AND BODY

Alcohol is classified as a depressant drug. After consuming alcohol, many users feel an initial effect that makes them feel relaxed, talkative, and confident. They may feel warm and slightly flushed. Then, if they drink more, the alcohol begins to slow the body's functions and reactions. They become sleepy, experience blurred vision, lose their balance, and have trouble thinking clearly. If they continue to drink, their speech becomes slurred, their breathing gets shallower, and their body temperature drops. They may lose consciousness. They may even stop breathing, which could lead to coma or death.

People with AUD can experience a number of respiratory problems.

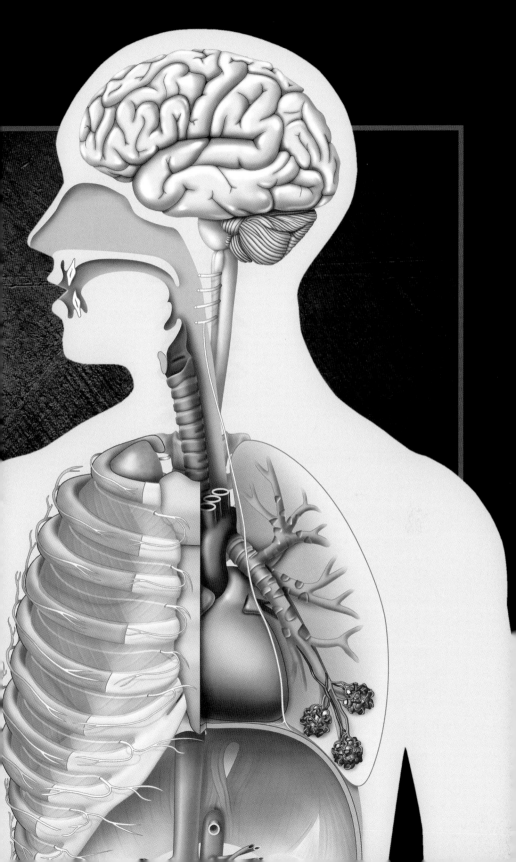

These effects are caused by chemical changes and reactions throughout the body and brain when alcohol is consumed. When someone drinks alcohol, a small amount of it moves directly through the stomach wall and into the bloodstream. The stomach breaks down some of the remaining alcohol, but most of it moves to the small intestine. From there, it goes into the bloodstream. A tiny bit of alcohol is exhaled in the breath and excreted in sweat, and a small amount is removed by the kidneys and excreted in urine. However, most of the

A depressant is a chemical that lowers the activity of vital organs such as the brain. Depressant drugs are sometimes called downers.

alcohol must be broken down by other organs. The liver plays a particularly vital role in removing alcohol from the bloodstream. Energy is released during this process. Approximately 200 calories are released per ounce of alcohol (30 mL).[1] These calories account for the food value of alcohol. However, they are considered empty calories because they don't contain any significant vitamins, minerals, or other nutrients. These empty calories can contribute to weight gain in people who consume a lot of alcohol and may result in the so-called beer belly.

BRAIN DRAIN

As alcohol moves into the bloodstream, it begins to affect many organs, especially the brain. The brain contains billions of nerve cells, or neurons. They communicate with each other using chemical messengers called neurotransmitters. These neurotransmitters travel across synapses—tiny spaces between neurons—to bind to other neurons. They either stimulate or slow the neurons' activity. The movement of these neurotransmitters is affected by the presence of alcohol. This causes a change in brain activity that makes a person feel pleasure and relaxation. These feelings contribute to the addictive properties of alcohol, as the brain wants to recapture the feelings again and again.

As more alcohol is consumed, the alcohol shuts down more and more brain circuits, making users feel mellow, sleepy, and withdrawn. Their fine motor coordination is affected during this stage. This affects reaction time and behavior, as well as bodily functions such as hearing, speech, and vision. However, the user doesn't necessarily recognize these changes. According to Dr. Akikur Mohammad, a professor at the University of Southern California, "Alcohol increases confidence but reduces performance. You do

EAST ASIANS AND ALCOHOL

More than one-third of all East Asians (Koreans, Japanese, and Chinese) lack an enzyme known as aldehyde dehydrogenase 2, which helps to break down alcohol in the body. As a result, drinking alcohol can cause them to experience facial flushing, nausea, and a rapid heart rate. People who lack this enzyme and continue to consume alcohol are at higher risk for cancer of the esophagus.

Alcohol can irritate the stomach and cause a person to vomit.

everything worse on alcohol, and everyone knows it except the person on alcohol."[2] At this stage, the drinker may also feel confused, dizzy, or aggressive.

As the effects of alcohol wear off and the euphoric feelings fade, people sometimes drink even more in an effort to regain the feelings. But this can be dangerous. It is easy for alcohol users to consume too much alcohol and cause themselves serious injury or even death. The body can process about one standard-sized serving of beer, wine, or spirits per hour. So if alcohol is consumed faster than that, it continues to build up in the brain and in other tissues—even after the person stops drinking.

As the brain shuts down functions, breathing slows. The muscles that close the trachea, or windpipe, when swallowing may also become paralyzed. If a person vomits during this time, the vomit may be inhaled into the lungs, causing inflammation, infection, or death.

BLOOD ALCOHOL CONCENTRATION

The amount of alcohol consumption required to cause fatal alcohol poisoning varies by body size and the speed at which it is consumed. A person's level of consumption is measured as blood alcohol concentration (BAC). A device commonly known as a Breathalyzer can be used to quickly gauge a person's BAC. The user simply blows into a tube, and the device analyzes the gases he or she exhales to determine his or her BAC.

A BAC above 0.35 (350 mg/dL) on a Breathalyzer machine is in the danger zone. This level could be reached by consuming

ALCOHOL AND THE BRAIN

Alcohol binds to receptors in the brain and mimics the effects of a neurotransmitter called GABA. GABA prevents the activity of neurons in brain circuits and regulates impulses. This initially makes drinkers feel relaxed and less inhibited. Eventually, as they become intoxicated, they may find themselves doing things that they would never consider doing while sober. Alcohol also inhibits a neurotransmitter called glutamate, slowing the activity of neurons and thus the user's thoughts, speech, and movement. Dopamine is another neurotransmitter affected by drinking alcohol. This chemical gives people a sense of well-being and pleasure. Several other neurotransmitters are affected by alcohol as well.

four 2-ounce (60 mL) shots of strong bourbon or 6.5 beers in one hour for a 100-pound (45 kg) female. An average 150-pound (68 kg) male would reach this BAC after seven shots of bourbon or twelve beers in one hour.[3]

These conditions frequently take place during drinking challenges or drinking games. Racing to drink or showing off for peers can result in dangerous situations. Another common cause is mixing alcohol with food or drinks that cover up its flavor, such as combining a hard liquor with a sugary juice or soda. Many times, the person consuming such a drink doesn't realize how much alcohol he or she is ingesting.

A BAC of just 0.03 (30 mg/dL) can slow reflexes and reaction times.[6] It can also impair alertness, vision, and the ability to discern sensory signals.

Within 20 minutes of taking a drink, a user's BAC begins to rise. This affects the brain's nerve cells, changing the person's feelings and behavior. A BAC of just 0.05 (50 mg/dL) can impair driving ability.[4] However, most people at this level do not appear to be intoxicated. The legal limit for driving is 0.08 (80 mg/dL) in most states.[5]

An average male weighing 140 pounds (64 kg) would be legally drunk, making it illegal to drive, after consuming three drinks in one hour, while a female of the same weight would be drunk after just over two drinks. For people under 21, there is a zero tolerance limit—even the slightest BAC can result in an arrest for driving under the influence (DUI) or driving while impaired (DWI). The usage of these terms varies by state. People with a BAC of more than 0.5 (500 mg/dL) usually stop breathing and die, but this can also occur at a lower BAC depending on their weight and gender, the number of drinks they had, how fast they consumed them, and the amount of food they ate.[7]

MIXING DRUGS AND ALCOHOL

Many sleep, depression, or anxiety medications, allergy drugs, some cold medicines, and illegal drugs are extremely dangerous to mix with alcohol. There are several reasons for this. When alcohol is present, the liver may break down medications faster or slower than normal. The medication may have toxic effects at a high concentration, or it may not work properly if it is broken down too quickly. The effects of alcohol and other

CAN ALCOHOL BE GOOD FOR YOU?

Some studies say that alcohol can be healthy when used in moderation by adults. Healthy moderation is defined as up to one standard drink per day for women and two standard drinks per day for men. In men, studies have shown that two standard drinks per day can slightly decrease the risk of heart disease, stroke, and diabetes by increasing high-density lipoprotein cholesterol—also known as good cholesterol— and reducing plaque in the arteries. Moderate alcohol use has also been shown to slow blood clotting. The effect is most noticeable for adults who are middle aged and older. However, the negative effects of heavy alcohol use outweigh any potential positives.

depressant drugs can also combine to slow bodily functions to much lower levels than expected. Thus a normal amount of alcohol can become deadly.

EFFECTS OF HEAVY ALCOHOL USE

Drinking large quantities of alcohol can impair short-term memory. Some people experience blackouts—periods when they are unable to remember anything that happened during or after they were drinking. Blackouts occur because short-term memories are blocked from being transferred to long-term storage. Drinking at a faster rate makes blackouts more likely.

Approximately 75 percent of people will experience uncomfortable symptoms, commonly known as a hangover, within hours after a bout of heavy drinking. These symptoms may include shakiness, nausea, headache, fatigue, and diarrhea. It takes anywhere from three to six drinks to produce a hangover, depending on the person's body size and gender.[8]

Heavy drinking can also lead to a dangerous condition known as alcohol poisoning. Symptoms of alcohol poisoning include vomiting, seizures, slow breathing, confusion, pale or bluish skin, low body temperature, unconsciousness, and even coma. Alcohol poisoning can be fatal if immediate medical care is not provided. According to the Centers for Disease Control and Prevention (CDC), more than 2,200 people die of alcohol poisoning in the United States every year—more than six per day.[9]

A person with severe AUD may suffer from serious withdrawal symptoms if he or she does not consume alcohol for a period of time. Symptoms of withdrawal include sleep problems, memory loss, and changes in mood and energy. Other potential symptoms include anxiety, nightmares, and paranoia. Some patients with severe alcohol withdrawal will experience trembling hands and arms, high blood pressure and pulse rate, sweating, sensitivity to noise and light, and hallucinations. These symptoms are known as delirium tremens (DTs). Left untreated, DTs can be fatal. It is critical for people with AUD to seek medical help for their condition.

DIFFERENT SIZES, DIFFERENT EFFECTS

Alcohol affects people differently. One person may be able to consume several drinks without severe effects, while another might drink the same amount and pass out. Body weight, gender, and metabolism all play a role in how quickly the body can process alcohol. Alcohol affects women more strongly in general. A woman weighing the same as a man will experience a stronger effect more quickly after consuming the same amount of alcohol. Women's bodies contain a lower percentage of water to dilute the alcohol, and they have smaller amounts of liver enzymes to break down alcohol. Another factor affecting the absorption of alcohol is the amount a person consumes and the alcohol's strength. In general, eating food with alcohol dilutes it and slows the reaction.

REWARD PATHWAY IN THE BRAIN

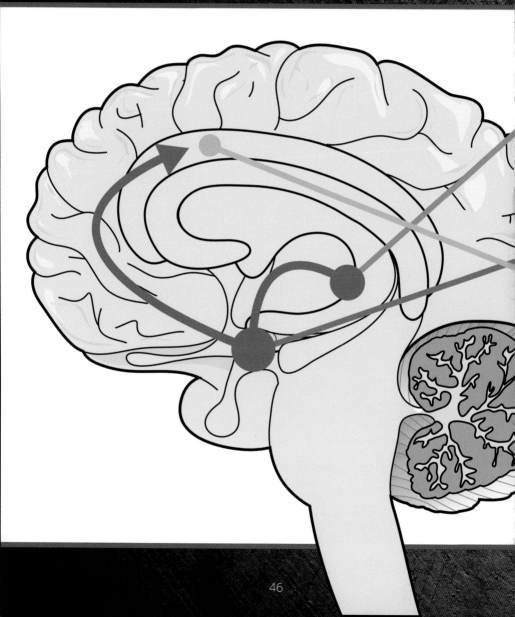

The reward pathway tells people to repeat a pleasurable action. This pathway is critical to understanding how addictions are formed.

VENTRAL TEGMENTAL AREA (VTA)

The VTA has neurons that mostly produce dopamine. Dopamine is a neurotransmitter that's released when people drink alcohol. Dopamine gives people a feeling of pleasure.

NUCLEUS ACCUMBENS

The nucleus accumbens receives dopamine from the VTA. The nucleus accumbens tells the brain what is pleasant.

PREFRONTAL CORTEX

The prefrontal cortex receives the information from the nucleus accumbens. The prefrontal cortex is responsible for reasoning and decision-making. The feeling of pleasure from dopamine will reinforce the behavior that caused it to be released. If drug or alcohol use leads to the release of dopamine, the reinforcement can cause people to form an addiction to the pleasurable substance.

LONG-TERM EFFECTS OF ALCOHOL USE

Author F. Scott Fitzgerald once said, "First you take a drink, then the drink takes a drink, then the drink takes you."[1] While some people can seemingly drink without ill effect, approximately 15 percent of people who drink alcohol will become addicted, which is known as AUD.[2] However, not all individuals who drink heavily are equally likely

The liver is one organ that can be severely damaged by alcohol.

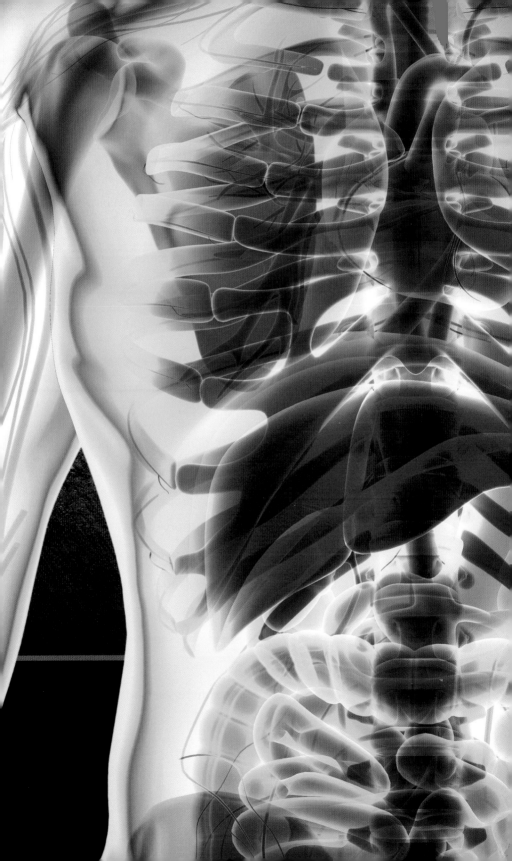

to develop AUD. Various environmental and genetic factors affect the likelihood of addiction.

The CDC reported in 2010 that 18.2 million people in the United States had AUD.[3] According to the National Institute on Alcohol Abuse and Alcoholism (NIAAA), the cost of alcohol misuse totaled $249 billion in 2010.[4] These expenses include accidents, injuries, property destruction, premature death, lost productivity, and crime-related expenses.

WHAT CAUSES AUD?

Throughout the 1900s, scientists argued about whether AUD was caused by genes or childhood experiences. As it turns out, both ideas were correct. There are a number of factors involved in the development of AUD, including a person's genetic makeup, environmental experience, and family history of AUD. People whose relatives abuse alcohol are more likely to also abuse alcohol. Genetic factors may make some people feel the effects of alcohol more strongly or make them more impulsive and prone to taking risks.

IS THERE AN ADDICTION GENE?

Several genes seem to play a role in alcohol addiction. However, there is not one specific gene that experts can point to as being responsible for addiction. Family history of AUD is a significant risk factor, and heavy alcohol use can permanently rewire a person's brain to cause addiction. Other experiences and environmental factors, such as where an individual lives, can influence the likelihood of addiction as well.

Certain early childhood experiences can also make people more likely to develop AUD. An unstable family situation and high levels of stress can influence brain development in a way that leads to poor impulse control and an inability to regulate emotions. These conditions can make people more prone to addiction. People experiencing stress as teens or adults sometimes respond by drinking excessively as well. However, most children of people with AUD do not develop the disorder themselves.

Heavy alcohol consumption can affect a person's appearance. It contributes to skin aging, dry, brittle hair and nails, and weight problems.

Symptoms of AUD include the inability of an individual to control how much he drinks, continuing to drink despite harmful effects, alcohol cravings, a high level of alcohol tolerance, and constantly thinking about the next drink. These are symptoms of changes in the brain that make a person drink compulsively. The more dependent an individual is on alcohol, the more likely it is that she will continue drinking even when she experiences negative consequences. Some people may need professional treatment to overcome their addiction.

Even years after a person with AUD stops drinking, he runs the risk of relapse. Stress, mood changes, and exposure to people, places, or things associated with drinking can trigger the craving for alcohol. This is due to changes in an addicted person's

Surgeons can remove diseased livers in a procedure known as a hepatectomy.

brain that cause it to respond to stress differently than the brain of a nonaddicted person.

The development of AUD is complex. Both environmental and genetic factors can play a role, and not every child of an addicted person will struggle with addiction. However, being aware of these risk factors can empower people at high risk for AUD to make better choices that reduce their chances of developing an addiction.

DISEASES LINKED TO HEAVY ALCOHOL CONSUMPTION

Long-term heavy alcohol consumption is linked to many different diseases. These include alcohol liver disease, heart disease, osteoporosis (a weakening of the bones), obesity, and damage to tooth enamel. Heavy alcohol use is linked to several types of cancer, especially cancers of the mouth and throat.

It also increases the risk of stomach, colon, rectal, liver, breast, and ovarian cancer. Increases in blood pressure associated with heavy alcohol use can increase the risk of heart attack or stroke as well.

Liver disease is one of the most common diseases caused by heavy alcohol use. Three different liver diseases are sometimes referred to as alcoholic liver disease. They are fatty liver, alcoholic hepatitis, and cirrhosis. Cirrhosis is a particularly deadly disease. It occurs when scar tissue forms on the liver. Scar tissue is developed when the liver is damaged. The liver can be damaged from too much exposure to alcohol. This scar tissue keeps the liver from functioning properly. Symptoms of cirrhosis range from fatigue, nausea, and itchy skin to internal bleeding and even liver failure and brain damage. Women's bodies are more likely to suffer liver damage than men's. This is because their bodies are lighter and have a higher fat-to-water ratio. Cirrhosis patients may eventually need a liver transplant, but they must remain alcohol free for at least six months before they will be considered for a transplant in many hospitals.

There is some evidence that drinking no more than one glass of wine per day for women or two glasses a day for men can lower the risk of heart disease. Grape skins produce antioxidant chemicals that help increase good cholesterol, and moderate consumption may help people relax. However, consuming large amounts of alcohol can result in serious damage to the heart and may lead to heart disease, heart failure, or cardiac arrest.

LONG-TERM EFFECTS ON THE BRAIN

Studies show that the brains of people who use alcohol heavily shrink in volume at a rate that varies with age and the amount of alcohol consumed. Alcohol keeps information from being processed efficiently in the brain, making the brain work harder to perform its necessary tasks. Alcohol also kills nerve cells and prevents new ones from being created.

The quantity and frequency of alcohol consumption, the age people start drinking, their current age, genetics, family history, and many other factors affect the impact of heavy drinking on the brain. Headaches, blackouts, and numbness in the hands and feet are some of the first symptoms of alcohol-related brain damage. Learning and memory problems as a result of heavy alcohol use may result directly from the presence of alcohol in the brain or indirectly

ALCOHOL AND THE HEART

The relationship between alcohol and heart health is complex. While some studies show a lower risk of heart attacks and fatal heart disease among moderate drinkers compared with people who don't drink, heavy alcohol use can damage the heart. Drinking too much can increase fats called triglycerides in the blood as well as blood pressure, therefore increasing the risk of heart disease. The excess calories consumed in alcohol can lead to obesity, another factor that increases the risk of heart disease. Heavy alcohol use can lead to irregular heartbeats and even heart failure or cardiac arrest.

from poor general health or liver disease. For example, the majority of people with alcohol addictions suffer a deficiency of thiamine (vitamin B1). This vitamin is found naturally in foods such as meat, whole-grain cereals, nuts, and dried beans. It is added as a supplement to many other foods, such as breads and cereals. Thiamine deficiency can lead to brain disorders such as Wernicke-Korsakoff syndrome (WKS). WKS can result in confusion, paralysis of the nerves that move the eyes, and lack of coordination. It usually causes long-term memory loss and learning problems as well.

The term *alcoholism* was coined by Swedish physician Magnus Huss in 1849.

Fortunately, the body is good at healing itself when given the opportunity. Most individuals with long-term heavy alcohol consumption will experience significant improvements in brain function after they stop drinking. Over time, some memory, thinking, and learning problems can be reversed as long as the person continues to abstain from alcohol.

ALCOHOL'S HARMFUL EFFECTS

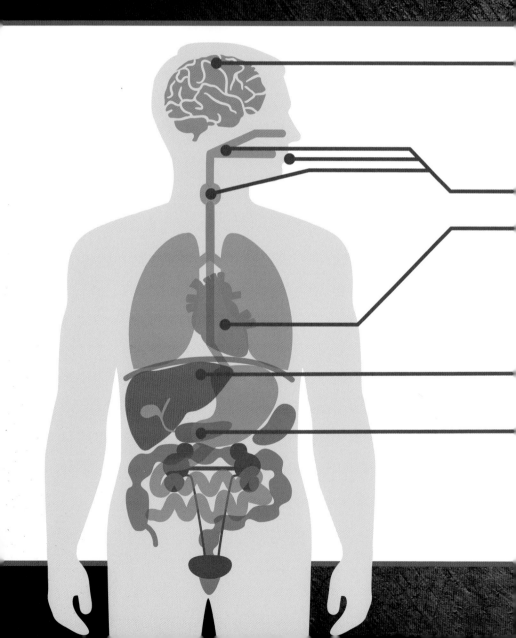

BRAIN

When alcohol enters the body, it disrupts the brain's natural processes. It impacts the communication pathways in the brain and can change the way people feel and behave. People who drink are less likely to think clearly and their coordination worsens.

THROAT
MOUTH
ESOPHAGUS

Consuming too much alcohol can increase a person's risk of cancers in the mouth, esophagus, and throat.

HEART

Drinking too much can damage the heart. People can experience irregular heartbeats and their heart muscle can stretch or droop. They can also suffer from high blood pressure or experience a stroke.

LIVER

Alcohol can severely impact the liver. It can cause issues including:
• Cirrhosis
• Alcoholic hepatitis, which is liver inflammation. People who have alcoholic hepatitis can experience a yellowing of the whites of the eyes and of the skin. They can also have nausea, weight loss, fever, fatigue, and a loss of appetite.
• A fatty liver, which is also known as hepatic steatosis. This can cause the liver to become inflamed and can sometimes lead to cirrhosis.

PANCREAS

Drinking alcohol can cause the pancreas to become dangerously inflamed. It can also make the blood vessels in the pancreas swell. This can hurt an individual's digestive process.

YOUNG ADULT ALCOHOL USE

Despite its potentially harmful effects, alcohol is the most widely used drug among teens and young adults in the United States. In a 2015 study, 20 percent of people aged 12 to 20 reported that they drank alcohol, and 13 percent had engaged in binge drinking within the previous 30 days.[1] Approximately 623,000 US youth aged 12 to 17 have AUD. Only about 5.2 percent of these have received treatment.[2]

Many ads for alcoholic beverages target young people. These ads try to normalize drinking while making it appear fun and appealing. University administrators and parents sometimes seem to look the other way when it comes to underage drinking,

Drinking has negative effects on a teen's brain

and some young people get around the minimum drinking age law by asking older friends or siblings to purchase alcohol for them.

Young people choose to drink for a variety of different reasons. According to the NIAAA, for many people peer pressure plays a big role. Some are seeking thrills or expect that drinking will be pleasurable. Other factors, such as genetics, advertising, and family views on alcohol consumption, also play a role.

Besides the fact that underage drinking is illegal, there are many health and safety reasons for people under the age of 21 to abstain from alcohol entirely. One of the biggest reasons is that alcohol affects young people's brains more severely than those of adults, in both the short term and the long term.

Adolescents appear to be less affected than adults by the short-term effects of alcohol on motor coordination, and they do not become sleepy as fast. However, alcohol has more impact on their memory. Because these warning signs of intoxication do not appear as quickly, adolescents may be more likely to drink to the point of danger or attempt to drive while impaired.

According to the NIAAA, "Evidence suggests that the most reliable predictor of a youth's drinking behavior is the drinking behavior of his or her friends."[3]

Drinking at a young age can have serious long-term consequences. Early drinking increases the risk of developing AUD. A study showed that 47 percent of adults who started drinking before the age of 14 developed AUD at some point in their lives, as compared with only 9 percent of those who waited to begin drinking until age 21.[4] In addition, heavy alcohol use can delay puberty in girls and lower testosterone in boys, affecting their physical growth and development.

Underage drinkers, especially those who engage in binge drinking, often experience problems with school attendance, grades, and relationships. And alcohol use can put young people into dangerous situations. A 2015 survey of high school youth found that during the 30 days before the survey, 20 percent had ridden in a car with someone who had been drinking and 8 percent had gotten behind the wheel after drinking alcohol.[5] As with adults, alcohol use increases the risk of suicide, drowning, violence, falls, burns, and many other types of injuries for young adults. Rates of sexual assault and high-risk sexual activity are also much higher among young adults who drink.

EFFECTS ON THE BRAIN

Studies show that alcohol consumption can rewire and damage young people's brains permanently. This is because

ADDRESSING THE PROBLEM

Young adults who feel that they have a problem with drinking should talk to a trusted adult and share their concerns. This might be a family member, teacher, guidance counselor, or religious leader. Many types of treatment and support groups are available. It is important not to wait until the problem gets out of control to do something about it. It's much easier to treat AUD before it becomes severe.

the brain is not fully developed until the mid to late 20s. When the brain is repeatedly exposed to alcohol or other drugs during adolescence, it can result in changes in the brain's structure.

Drinking during adolescence may reduce the size of the hippocampus, a portion of the brain associated with learning and memory. Studies on animals have shown that alcohol inhibits a brain chemical that affects the ability to learn. Alcohol also impairs the prefrontal areas of the brain, which are responsible for controlling impulses and thinking through the consequences of an action before performing it. This impairment can lead to dangerous situations and unwise choices. Young people who use alcohol heavily have smaller volumes of white matter, or bundles of nerve fibers, in their brains, which can lead to symptoms of depression. They also have reduced blood flow to the brain, which increases the risk of suffering a stroke.

BINGE DRINKING

Either as a result of peer pressure or in an effort to get drunk as quickly as possible and lose their inhibitions, some people consume large amounts of alcohol very quickly. This is known as binge drinking. Binge drinking can be defined in various ways, but the NIAAA defines it as "a pattern of drinking that brings blood alcohol concentration (BAC) levels to 0.08 g/dL [80 mg/dL]."[6] This generally means four drinks for women or five drinks for men in a span of two hours. Many young binge drinkers consume considerably more than this amount. Those who engage in binge drinking five or more times per month are considered heavy alcohol users.

Binge drinking is a serious problem in the United States. It is particularly common among people younger than 21, accounting for 90 percent of all alcohol consumption by this group.[7] A study of college students involved in binge drinking found that 63 percent had done something that they later

The CDC has noted that binge drinking can lead to accidental injuries and death.

Getting involved in extracurricular activities is one way teens can avoid alcohol use.

regretted while intoxicated. Fifty-four percent had forgotten

where they were or what happened while they were drinking,

and 41 percent reported unplanned sexual activity. Twenty-two

percent engaged in unprotected sex, leading to the possibility of pregnancy or sexually transmitted diseases (STDs).[8]

Most of the causes of death associated with drinking in this age-group, such as unintentional injury, homicide, and suicide, are related to binge drinking. It is also associated with alcohol poisoning, car crashes, sexual assault, and academic problems.

The high levels of BAC associated with binge drinking can lead to a variety of physical problems as well. They can cause stroke, heart disease, and liver disease. They also increase the risk of STDs, diabetes, and certain types of cancer. Binge drinking has no health benefits.

PREVENTING UNDERAGE DRINKING

There are many approaches to preventing underage drinking. At the community level, raising the price of alcohol and enforcing stricter laws can lower rates of underage drinking. On an individual level, school- and family-based programs can be effective as well. School-based programs are aimed at setting healthier social norms, addressing peer pressure, and teaching resistance skills, while family-based programs work at improving communication, listening, and problem-solving skills within families.

MAKING GOOD CHOICES

All humans experience fear, loneliness, pain, and disappointment from time to time. Many people want to appear smart, funny, or outgoing. Drinking seems to offer a solution to these problems, but it is a short-term solution at best. At worst, it is a serious health and safety risk, in addition to being illegal for minors. The more alcohol a person drinks at a time, the more bodily functions shut down, putting the person at risk of alcohol poisoning or even death.

Saying no to dares or challenges and avoiding alcohol mixed in punch, Jell-O, or fizzy drinks that can hide high alcohol concentrations can help prevent dangerous levels of alcohol consumption. In addition, it is imperative that people avoid mixing alcohol with prescription or illegal drugs. The combination of drugs and alcohol can cause dangerous interactions. And calling a trusted person for help in a dangerous or awkward situation can be a lifesaver.

EVERYONE ISN'T DOING IT

Statistics show that the majority of Americans do not drink. The best way to avoid difficult situations is to choose friends who do not drink and to avoid events where people plan to drink. However, unexpected situations can arise. Experts suggest that young people come up with excuses in advance in case they are put into a situation where there is pressure to drink or to get into a car with someone who has been drinking. Putting the blame on parental rules or an upcoming athletic event are good options.

SOCIAL COSTS

When people abuse alcohol, their behavior affects not only themselves but also their family, friends, and even strangers. These negative effects can be referred to as social costs. The social costs of heavy alcohol consumption include drunk driving, violence and crime, family problems, and harmful effects on unborn children.

DRUNK DRIVING

A changing traffic light or a sudden stop by the car ahead requires drivers to react quickly. While people who have had several drinks may not feel drunk, their reaction times are slowed by the alcohol they have consumed. There is more time between when they see or hear something and the time they respond.

In 2017, high school students in Indiana watched a mock drunk driving incident. Junior Isabelle Dotlich participated in the event as the drunk driver. The police gave her a Breathalyzer test.

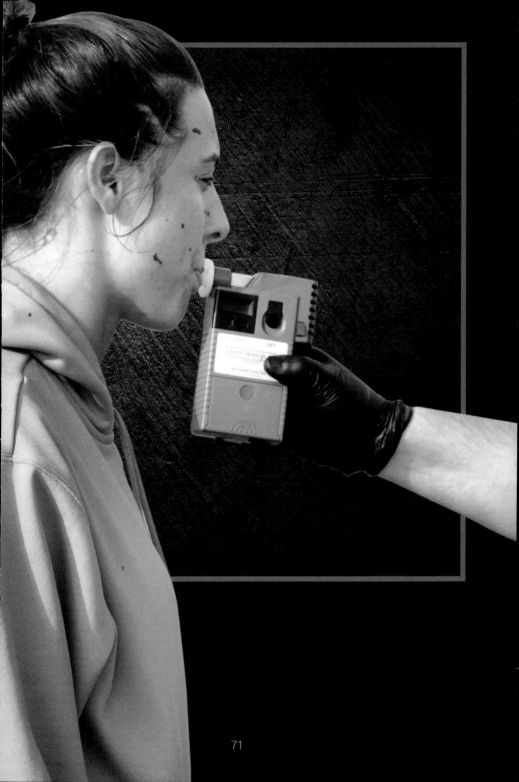

Drinking also makes a person's muscles less coordinated. As a result, driving under the influence of alcohol frequently leads to car crashes.

This is an issue that affects nearly everyone. It is estimated that two out of every three people will be affected by a drunk driving crash at some point in their lives.[1] Car crashes are the leading cause of death from injury in the United States, and the leading cause of death for people aged 15 to 34. Approximately one-half of these crashes are alcohol related.[2] One person in the United States dies almost every hour in an alcohol-related vehicle accident. This adds up to approximately 10,000 deaths per year. Approximately 290,000 more people are injured.[3]

Drinking affects people's judgment, making them less likely to make wise decisions about getting behind the wheel. So, it is critical for friends to step in if someone is too intoxicated to drive safely. In the words of

A HIGH-TECH SOLUTION TO DRUNK DRIVING

A cell phone–sized device can dramatically cut down on repeat drunk driving episodes when it is installed in the vehicles of people convicted of DUI or DWI. This device requires the driver to blow into a tube before the car will start. If alcohol is detected, it will prevent the car from starting. This device allows people with DUI convictions to drive while still preventing them from driving drunk. The CDC has found that this system can reduce repeat DUI offenses by two-thirds when it is implemented, potentially saving thousands of lives. Currently, 30 states require these devices for repeat offenders.[4]

the Ad Council's long-running anti–drunk driving campaign: "Friends don't let friends drive drunk!"[5]

GETTING MADD

Several organizations make it their mission to combat drunk driving and prevent alcohol- and drug-related traffic deaths. One of the best-known of these is Mothers Against Drunk Driving (MADD). This group's mission is to "end drunk driving, help fight drugged driving, support the victims of these violent crimes and prevent underage drinking."[6] Candace Lightner founded MADD in 1980, four days after her daughter, Cari, was killed by a drunk driver with multiple convictions on his record.

Within three years of its creation, MADD became an international organization with millions of members. The group provides support for victims, raises awareness of the issues drunk driving can cause, and advocates for new, stricter laws regarding drunk driving. This organization has been effective at changing societal attitudes on the issue of drunk driving.

A spin-off of MADD is known as Students Against Destructive Decisions (SADD). Founded in 1981, SADD empowers young people to help educate their peers about the dangers of

Because a motorcycle provides less protection to the driver than a car, getting on a motorcycle while drunk is even more dangerous than getting in a car. The number of motorcycle deaths in 2015 was nearly 29 times that of other vehicles per mile driven. Up to one-half of all motorcyclists killed in nighttime crashes have a BAC of 0.10 (100 mg/dL) or greater.[7]

During a MADD gathering, people held up pictures of their loved ones who were killed in drunk driving accidents.

substance abuse, drunk driving, and other issues. Its core focus is on traffic safety, but SADD programs also address substance abuse, depression, suicide, and teen violence and bullying, all of which can be related to heavy alcohol consumption and drunk driving.

VIOLENCE AND CRIME

Alcohol use is strongly associated with violence and crime. People who abuse alcohol are more likely to commit crimes. They are also more likely to be victims of rape, theft, and attacks.

Alcohol use is linked to 41.7 percent of violent crimes. More than one-third of all offenders in the criminal justice system were under the influence when they committed their crimes.[8] Alcohol is especially likely to be involved in violence between partners, such as spouses or people who are dating or living together.

Four out of every five arrests of children or teens involve alcohol or drugs.[9]

A study of youth who used alcohol showed that they were more likely to have behaved violently, destroyed property, or assaulted others in the past year. Youth who drink heavily are more likely to engage in shoplifting, drug trafficking, and other illegal activities. They are also more likely to consider or attempt suicide.

There are several possible reasons for the link between alcohol and violence. First, alcohol decreases a person's capacity for self-control, which affects both offenders and victims. It can also cause people to misread social cues and therefore overreact to any perceived threat. People under the influence of alcohol also may not be able to reasonably judge the risks of acting on their violent impulses. They may follow through on these

A GATEWAY TO CRIME

Alcohol and tobacco are sometimes referred to as gateway drugs. Gateway drugs are drugs that make experimentation with substances such as cocaine, heroin, marijuana, or methamphetamine more likely. Not only is possession of these drugs a crime but using them can make people more likely to commit other crimes. This may result from the effect of the drug on their thoughts and behavior, from trying to get money to fund their drug habit to producing or selling drugs.

impulses without thinking about the consequences. In addition, individuals who intend to commit violent acts may drink to boost their courage.

Being in a location where people are drinking, such as a bar or club, increases a person's risk of becoming a victim of violence. This is because people in the area may be more aggressive, friends may be less capable of protecting each other if they are drinking, and inhibitions may be lowered for people who are drinking.

UNPLANNED SEXUAL ACTIVITY

Because alcohol tends to lower inhibitions and affect judgment, it often leads people to engage in unplanned sexual activity.

Many adults drink alcohol as a social activity.

Alcohol also increases the likelihood of risky behaviors such as unprotected sexual intercourse and having multiple sexual partners.

This link is particularly strong among young people. A study by the National Center on Addiction and Substance Abuse showed that teens under the age of 15 who had ever had a drink were twice as likely to have had sexual intercourse than those who didn't drink. That number rose to seven times as likely for those aged 15 and up.[10]

Serious consequences may result, including unplanned pregnancies and exposure to STDs. Young adults who drink are twice as likely to contract an STD as those who do not drink, and the risk for heavy drinkers is even higher.

EFFECTS ON THE FAMILY

More than 10 percent of US children live with a parent who has an alcohol problem, according to an NIAAA study.[11] Another study found that one in four children is affected by heavy alcohol consumption or by AUD in the family.[12] These families are more likely to deal with violence, infidelity, economic insecurity, and divorce. Family conflict and unemployment are also associated with heavy drinking, and it can result in financial difficulties as well.

Among couples, heavy alcohol consumption tends to result in increased nagging, arguing, and domestic violence. This type

CHILDREN OF PEOPLE WITH AUD

Children of individuals with AUD face a unique set of problems. It is common for these children to feel high levels of stress, guilt, loneliness, helplessness, fear of abandonment, and depression. They often feel that they created their parents' problem in some way. Young children of people with AUD may experience bed-wetting, nightmares, and frequent crying. Older children often display symptoms of poor self-image, phobias, or obsessive perfectionism. Their school performance is often affected, and they are less likely to go to college. Children of individuals with AUD are also more likely to suffer child abuse. Many continue to experience problems in adulthood.

of conflict increases stress in the whole family. Alcohol-impaired parents tend to be inconsistent and unpredictable; they often lack clear rules and limits. They are also more likely to abuse or neglect their children.

Heavy alcohol consumption not only affects the user but can have direct consequences for unborn children as well. Alcohol can be extremely harmful to a fetus's development when a woman uses it during pregnancy. Alcohol can cross the placenta to reach the developing fetus and can keep oxygen and nutrients from reaching it. This can lead to a condition known as fetal alcohol syndrome (FAS). The rate of FAS in the United States is estimated at 1 case per 1,000 births.[13] Children born with FAS tend to have below-average intelligence and weigh less than average. A baby with FAS has distinct facial features including a thin upper lip, smooth philtrum—which is the groove above the lips—and

Pregnant women who drink alcohol are more likely to miscarry or deliver babies with low birth weights.

small eye openings, and he or she may suffer from problems with speech, hearing, learning, memory, problem-solving, and attention span. FAS is the leading cause of intellectual disability in the United States. People with FAS often have trouble in school and struggle to get along with others. There is no cure for this syndrome.

Although the link between a mother's alcohol use and damage to her child's health is well known, recent studies show that alcohol use by fathers may play a role as well. Offspring of male mice exposed to alcohol suffered abnormal brain and organ development. Researchers have found that FAS can be found in children whose mothers never drank alcohol, which suggests that their fathers' alcohol use may have been responsible.

CHAPTER EIGHT

LAWS AND POLICIES

Although Prohibition no longer exists, the government still regulates the sale and use of alcohol in the United States. Studies show that laws can be quite effective at reducing alcohol use, especially among minors.

Various policies can be effective at reducing heavy alcohol use and drunk driving. One of these is raising taxes. There is a clear relationship between taxes and alcohol consumption. When taxes on alcohol increase, alcohol consumption decreases, and vice versa. Other effective actions include setting BAC limits, creating sobriety checkpoints on the roads, and establishing

In 2017, Utah lawmakers lowered the DUI limit to a BAC of 0.05. Representative Norman Thurston sponsored the bill.

Ignition interlock devices can be installed in cars. They measure a person's BAC and can help prevent DUIs.

random breath testing stops for drivers. These actions help to deter people from driving while drunk.

DUI OR DWI

When drivers are suspected of driving under the influence of alcohol, police officers will often conduct a field sobriety test to check drivers' coordination. A driver may be asked to stand with one leg slightly off the ground for 30 seconds or take nine steps, heel to toe, in a straight line. Officers also look to check for involuntary jerking of the eyes when gazing to the side. While everyone's eyes do this to some extent, the jerking is exaggerated when a person is intoxicated. If a driver appears to be impaired, the officer may give her a Breathalyzer test. State laws regarding Breathalyzer tests vary, but drivers who refuse to take one may face consequences such as license suspensions or even jail time.

Being convicted of DUI or DWI can have serious consequences, including fines, jail time, loss of employment, and higher insurance rates. In addition, it can cause personal and family embarrassment.

UNDERAGE DRINKING

It's illegal in the United States for people under age 21 to purchase or consume alcohol. Alcohol use by people under this age is called underage drinking. There are good reasons for these laws. Thousands of young people die every year as a result of homicides, suicides, drownings, accidents, and injuries related to alcohol use.

ALCOHOL LAWS AROUND THE WORLD

Laws regarding alcohol use vary widely around the world. Sixteen Muslim countries ban alcohol entirely, although some of them make exceptions for non-Muslims. In contrast, 21 countries have no minimum legal drinking age.[1] The rest of the world's countries have a minimum legal drinking age ranging from 10 to 21. The United States is among those with the highest minimum legal drinking age, although a few parts of India have minimum legal drinking ages as high as 25 or 30.

Drunk driving is dangerous to the driver and to other people on the roads.

Laws setting the minimum drinking age at 21 were first put in place after Prohibition was repealed. However, between 1970 and 1975, many states lowered the drinking age to 18, 19, or 20 in response to the legal voting age being lowered to 18 during the Vietnam War (1955–1975). They reasoned that if soldiers were old enough to fight and vote, surely they were old enough to drink.

This change in the legal drinking age was followed by an increased number of problems related to alcohol, especially traffic deaths. Studies clearly show that a minimum legal drinking

age of 21 decreases both alcohol consumption and traffic deaths, especially among people under age 21. By 1976, most states had raised their minimum legal drinking age to 21 again. Because of the varied state laws, a new problem arose. Some teens would go to neighboring states with lower drinking ages to drink and then crash while driving home drunk.

To combat this issue, Congress decided to standardize the minimum drinking age. But rather than directly setting a federal minimum drinking age, the Uniform Drinking Age Act of 1984 threatened states with the loss of 10 percent of their federal highway funding if they did not raise their minimum drinking age to 21.[2] By 1988, all 50 states had complied, although some allowed exemptions for permission by a parent and religious activities.

Because it is illegal for people under 21 to purchase, possess, or consume alcohol, no BAC is acceptable when they are driving. To standardize laws about underage drinking and driving, Congress again used the threat of losing highway funds to encourage states to adopt zero tolerance laws under the National Highway Systems Designation Act of 1995. These laws set a BAC limit of 0.02 (20 mg/dL) for underage drivers.[3] Essentially, if any alcohol is found in an underage person's system, his or her license can be suspended or revoked. By 1998, all 50 states had zero tolerance laws. These laws immediately lowered the number of crashes, especially single-vehicle nighttime crashes.

MEDIA AND ADVERTISING

The advertising media has a complicated history with alcohol companies. Unlike cigarettes, alcoholic beverages are still advertised on TV, in magazines, and on the internet. Beverage companies also sponsor music festivals and sporting events, and they purchase Facebook ads, window displays for restaurants and stores, and product placements in movies and TV shows. Some even hire college students to pass out items with the company's logo. In 2010, the alcohol industry spent $1.7 billion on various types of ads.[4] Very few of the ads promoted responsible drinking, and those that did accounted for just over 2 percent of the alcohol industry's entire advertising budget.[5]

The advertising industry has agreed to avoid advertising in media where more than 28.4 percent of the audience is underage.[6] The industry has also agreed that ad content should not specifically target people under 21. However, many ads still target teens and the places and media they frequent. And many alcohol-industry websites offer games, contests, screen savers, and other promotions that appeal to young people. Humor, animal and human characters, and youth-oriented music

Many advertisers use colorful billboards to sell their products.

seem to be highly effective techniques. Alcohol ads are also frequently associated with sporting events that youth attend and watch on TV. One example is the popular Budweiser "Puppy Love" ad that was introduced during the 2014 Super Bowl.

A VOLUNTARY AGREEMENT

Why do alcohol ads appear on television, but not tobacco ads? Because of the First Amendment, which guarantees freedom of speech, the government cannot ban alcohol companies from advertising their products to young people. The agreement among the beverage companies is voluntary and unenforceable. The tobacco industry, by contrast, voluntarily agreed not to advertise in a number of different venues, including TV, after it was sued by 46 states in the 1990s.

Alcohol ads try to associate brands of alcohol with people who are cool, fun, and successful. The goal of these advertisers is profits. Because many people start drinking before the legal drinking age, the target audience for alcohol advertisers continues to get younger and younger. They want young people to become loyal to their products as soon as they start drinking. And advertising works. A 2016 study looked at the amount that people aged 13 to 20 drank and found that it was significantly affected by the number of alcohol ads they had viewed in the past year. Viewing those ads affected not only people's consumption of those brands but also their consumption of other brands as well. One study estimated that a ban on alcohol advertising would potentially result in more than 7,000 fewer alcohol-related deaths among the millions of people in their sample group.[7]

The best way for viewers to resist these ads is to look critically at them. Who is paying for the ad, and what are they trying to sell? What is the ad trying to make viewers believe? Does it try to make drinking look fun and cool? Does it show any of the negative effects of drinking this product?

Laws and policies can have a big impact on alcohol consumption patterns, especially among young people. Setting reasonable but strong laws and enforcing them consistently can cut down on alcohol-related injuries and deaths, leading to a safer and healthier society for all.

ALCOHOL ENERGY DRINK

In the 2000s, alcohol energy drinks, also known as caffeinated alcoholic beverages, were frequently marketed to teens. These drinks contained alcohol mixed with caffeine, sugar, and flavoring. In 2010, the Food and Drug Administration determined that these drinks were not safe, and companies were forced to remove their products from the market. Some of them simply removed the caffeine and other stimulants and continued to market their drinks.

However, some people continue to mix energy drinks with alcohol on their own, a practice that can be extremely dangerous. The effects of the caffeine make users feel more alert than they normally would and lead to a state known as wide-awake drunkenness. People who consume alcohol and energy drinks may not realize how drunk they are. One study found that students who consumed these drinks had double the risk of injury, sexual assault, and drunk driving incidents.

CHAPTER NINE

RECOVERING FROM ALCOHOL USE DISORDER

For people with AUD, the first step to overcoming their addiction is to realize that a problem exists. A variety of treatments are available. But for most people, a visit to the doctor or a self-help group such as AA is a good place to start. These steps may be sufficient for some people, but others need more intensive treatment. Options may include talk and drug therapy or a detoxification and rehabilitation program at home, in a hospital, or in a residential clinic.

AA published a book about recovering from alcohol addiction. ▶

Some people with AUD may be able to cut back their drinking to a moderate, healthier level. However, studies show that people who are addicted to alcohol are most successful when they stop drinking entirely rather than try to drink in moderation. This is because most people addicted to alcohol find themselves unable to stop with a drink or two. As author Richard Taite noted, "One drink gives the brain the leverage it needs to force the addicted person into many."[1]

MEDICATION TREATMENT

Certain types of medications can help people fighting AUD. Tranquilizers or beta-blockers relax the mind and body and can help make withdrawal symptoms more manageable. Other drugs work by helping to remove the desire to drink. They block cravings or even make people nauseous if they drink.

The most commonly used drugs in treating alcohol withdrawal are benzodiazepines, which include diazepam (Valium), chlordiazepoxide (Librium), lorazepam (Ativan), and oxazepam (Serax). These help minimize the symptoms of withdrawal. Disulfiram (Antabuse) works by making people feel sick if they drink alcohol. Other drugs help reduce cravings for alcohol. Some of them reduce the high that drinkers feel when they consume alcohol. Instead of feeling euphoric, they feel sluggish.

Drug therapies can be very helpful, but they do not replace other types of therapies or support groups. The Food and Drug Administration specifically states that they should only be prescribed to patients who are receiving other types of therapy. One downside of drug therapies is that they only work if the patient takes the drug reliably. Combining them with other therapies may lead to better outcomes.

Valium can be used to treat anxiety.

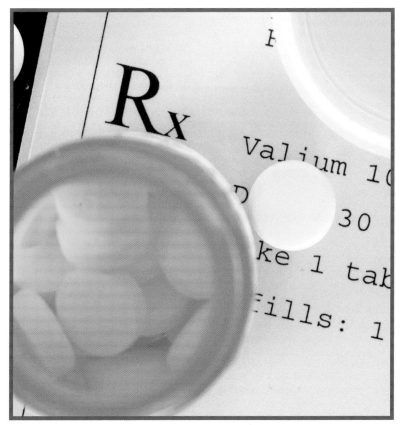

BEHAVIORAL TREATMENT

Many people drink because they feel socially excluded or alienated from others. This emotional pain and stress causes damage to the neurological system and can increase the likelihood of addiction. Therapists can help people identify chronic stress factors in their life and learn to deal with them in healthy ways. Emotionally meaningful experiences can create new neurons and pathways and change brain function. These changes in brain biology can change the way people think, feel, and act. Making good choices about nutrition and exercise can help in dealing with stress as well.

Cognitive behavioral therapy (CBT) is one of the best-known types of treatment for AUD. This type of therapy is based on the idea that an individual's own current thoughts and behaviors, rather than other people or past events or situations, cause them to feel or behave in certain ways. While people can't always change their situation, they can change how they think and feel about it and develop behavioral skills for future actions. CBT involves helping people think about their drinking and the choices they make concerning it. In this model, therapists help their clients think about healthier ways to address their needs and avoid triggers that tempt them to drink. CBT is sometimes combined with naltrexone, a drug that helps reduce the craving for alcohol.

Motivational enhancement therapy (MET) is another approach. It involves counseling sessions employing a motivational interviewing style between the therapist and patient. MET is aimed at helping the patient to get motivated for change and to stay committed to change. As with CBT, this type of therapy may be combined with medication to increase its effectiveness.

ALTERNATIVE THERAPIES

While medication, CBT, and support groups are the best-known treatments for AUD, studies show that some alternative therapies can be effective as well. Among these are yoga and meditation. These relaxation practices can help rewire the brain to deal with stress and anxiety in healthier ways, thereby decreasing the odds that a person will resort to alcohol use to deal with these feelings. Yoga also has a positive impact on sleep and dietary choices, which can help lower stress.

SUPPORT GROUPS

Many people find the support of others recovering from AUD to be invaluable in helping them stay sober. The best known support group for people with this disorder is AA, which started in 1935 and now has chapters in more than 180 countries.[3] AA asks members to follow a 12-step program that begins with admitting alcohol has control of their lives, making lists of people they've harmed by drinking, and making amends to the best of their ability. It also emphasizes spiritual growth,

Members of AA often mark significant achievements in remaining sober with specially engraved tokens, medallions, or chips.

There are many activities people can do besides drinking, such as watching a movie.

personal responsibility, and helping other people with AUD. AA groups reference a higher power, but the organization is not specifically religious.

AA meetings are free and open to all. Members remain anonymous, and anything shared at the meetings is confidential.

Studies have shown AA to be an effective part of long-term recovery. It has helped hundreds of thousands of people to become and remain sober.

A 2008 study suggested that 3 to 3.5 percent of US adults have attended one or more AA meetings, and nearly 80 percent of people seeking help for AUD participate in AA.[4]

Because not everyone feels comfortable with AA's emphasis on a higher power, some secular organizations have sprung up as well. Some of the best known of these are Secular Organization for Sobriety, SMART Recovery, and Women for Sobriety.

Al-Anon is another support group that helps the families and friends of people with AUD. A separate branch of this group, called Alateen, is specifically geared toward teenagers in this situation. Another group is called Adult Children of Alcoholics.

STAGING AN INTERVENTION

Sometimes when a person is not willing to admit that he has an alcohol problem, his family or friends will gather to have a serious conversation with him. This conversation is known as an intervention.

REHABILITATION OPTIONS

Rehabilitation, or rehab, programs offer intensive treatment for those with AUD. Some are inpatient and are held in a hospital or clinic. Others allow the patient to live at home and visit a clinic for treatment. This is known as outpatient treatment. In some cases, patients choose to enter rehab, and in other cases, they may be ordered to enter a program by the court after being convicted of an alcohol-related crime. Programs may have a religious or a secular basis.

In extreme cases, where quitting alcohol could cause serious harm, the patients may need to go through detoxification. Because sudden withdrawal from alcohol can cause life-threatening symptoms, it is important for patients to detox under medical supervision. This process can take up to ten days. Drug therapies can help ease withdrawal symptoms.

KNOW THE RISKS

Alcohol is legal for adults and plays important roles in cultural life in the United States. However, many people use alcohol in unhealthy or dangerous ways. For those who choose to drink, it is important to understand the risks associated with AUD and know how to drink responsibly and avoid harm. It is also important for people to know that if they have a family

NEW TREATMENTS ON THE HORIZON

No one treatment for AUD is effective for everyone, and often a combination of treatments are used. Researchers continue to search for new drugs that can help patients overcome AUD. One experimental drug that shows promise is called ABT-436. This drug works by blocking the effects of vasopressin, a hormone that regulates feelings of stress and anxiety. Since people with AUD often drink when they are faced with stressful situations, researchers hope that this drug will make them less likely to do so.

history of AUD, they are more likely to develop alcohol problems. Alcohol consumption is not only illegal for people under age 21 but can cause serious legal, physical, mental, and emotional problems for young people.

Support groups can help people who are in recovery from addiction.

ESSENTIAL FACTS

EFFECTS ON THE BODY

- Alcohol affects the brain as well as other organs in the body. It acts as a depressant, slowing reaction times and bodily functions.

- Drinking too much alcohol at one time can lead to severe effects such as alcohol poisoning and even death. It raises the risk of unwanted sexual activity, drowning, vehicle accidents, and violence.

- Long-term abuse of alcohol can damage the brain, liver, heart, and other organs. One common condition is cirrhosis of the liver, which results from scar tissue formed in the liver by exposure to alcohol. This disease keeps the liver from functioning properly.

- For some people, heavy alcohol consumption can also lead to alcohol use disorder (AUD). People with severe AUD continue drinking alcohol despite the serious problems it causes them and the ways in which it affects others.

LAWS AND POLICIES

- Laws in the United States prohibit anyone under the age of 21 from buying or drinking alcohol. Other laws prohibit driving with a blood alcohol concentration (BAC) of more than 0.08 (80 mg/dL). Zero tolerance laws make it illegal for drivers under the age of 21 to drive with a BAC of more than 0.02 (20 mg/dL).

- Advertising for alcoholic beverages is pervasive in US culture. Advertisers are not supposed to target audiences that consist of more than 28.4 percent underage people, but many find ways around this policy.

IMPACT ON SOCIETY

Heavy alcohol consumption costs the United States billions of dollars each year. Some of these costs stem from alcohol-related crime, illnesses, and injuries, including motor vehicle accidents. Other costs result from decreased productivity at work due to alcohol-related illnesses. However, the impact of heavy alcohol consumption goes beyond the economic costs. It negatively affects family relationships and even harms the next generation by causing fetal alcohol syndrome, a condition that affects the mental and physical development of children.

QUOTE

"Alcohol increases confidence but reduces performance. You do everything worse on alcohol, and everyone knows it except the person on alcohol."

—Dr. Akikur Mohammad, professor at the University of Southern California

GLOSSARY

ABSTINENCE
The practice of not doing or having something that is desired, such as drinking alcohol.

ADDICTION
A compulsive need for a habit-forming substance, such as nicotine or alcohol.

DETOXIFICATION
A treatment process in which a person with a drug addiction abstains from taking a drug and doctors administer medications to help the individual's body adjust to not having the drug.

DISTILL
To purify a liquid by boiling it, collecting the steam, and letting it cool.

ENZYME
A protein that helps break down other chemicals in the body.

FERMENTATION
The process of chemical change, often involving yeast or microorganisms, that results in the production of alcohol.

INHIBITION
A mental restraint on a person's behavior or speech.

NEURON
A cell that sends messages from the body to the brain and vice versa; a nerve cell.

NEUROTRANSMITTER
A brain chemical that helps brain cells communicate with other brain cells.

RELAPSE
A recurrence of a disease or other ailment after it seems to have been conquered or cured.

SOBRIETY
The state of being sober; not under the influence of alcohol or mind-altering drugs.

YEAST
A small, single-celled fungus that breaks down sugars in grains, fruits, or vegetables to form alcohol.

ADDITIONAL RESOURCES

SELECTED BIBLIOGRAPHY

Chrzan, Janet. *Alcohol: Social Drinking in Cultural Context*. New York: Routledge, 2013. Print.

Mohammad, Akikur. *The Anatomy of Addiction*. New York: Perigee, 2016. Print.

Rose, Mark E. *Alcohol: Its History, Pharmacology, and Treatment*. Center City, MN: Hazelden, 2011. Print.

FURTHER READINGS

Bow, James. *Binge Drinking*. New York: Crabtree, 2015. Print.

Burlingame, Jeff. *Alcohol*. New York: Marshall Cavendish Benchmark, 2013. Print.

ONLINE RESOURCES

Booklinks
NONFICTION NETWORK
FREE! ONLINE NONFICTION RESOURCES

To learn more about alcohol, visit **abdobooklinks.com.** These links are routinely monitored and updated to provide the most current information available.

MORE INFORMATION

For more information on this subject, contact or visit the following organizations:

ALCOHOLICS ANONYMOUS

A.A. World Services, Inc.
PO Box 459
Grand Central Station
New York, NY 10163
212-870-3400
aa.org

This international organization provides support for people recovering from AUD.

NATIONAL INSTITUTE ON ALCOHOL ABUSE AND ALCOHOLISM

5635 Fishers Lane, MSC 9304
Bethesda, MD 20892-9304
301-443-3860
niaaa.nih.gov

The NIAAA is part of the National Institutes of Health. It supports and conducts alcohol-related research in a variety of fields. This information is shared with policymakers, the health-care industry, and the public.

SOURCE NOTES

CHAPTER 1. A SERIOUS PROBLEM

1. Helaina Hovitz. "How I Knew I Needed to Stop Drinking Alcohol." *Teen Vogue*. Condé Nast, 29 June 2017. Web. 20 Feb. 2018.
2. Hovitz, "How I Knew I Needed to Stop Drinking Alcohol."
3. Mark E. Rose. *Alcohol: Its History, Pharmacology, and Treatment*. Center City, MN: Hazelden, 2011. Print. 9.
4. "Fact Sheets—Alcohol Use and Your Health." *Centers for Disease Control and Prevention*. US Department of Health & Human Services, n.d. Web. 20 Feb. 2018.
5. "Alcohol Facts and Statistics." *National Institute on Alcohol Abuse and Alcoholism*. US Department of Health & Human Services, June 2017. Web. 20 Feb. 2018.
6. "Alcohol Facts and Statistics."
7. "CAGE Questionnaire." *National Institute on Alcohol Abuse and Alcoholism*. US Department of Health & Human Services, Feb. 2002. Web. 20 Feb. 2018.
8. "Alcohol Facts and Statistics."
9. "Facing Addiction in America." *Surgeon General.gov*. US Department of Health & Human Services, Nov. 2016. Web. 20 Feb. 2018.

CHAPTER 2. HOW ALCOHOL IS MADE

1. "What Is a Standard Drink?" *National Institute on Alcohol Abuse and Alcoholism*. US Department of Health & Human Services, n.d. Web. 20 Feb. 2018.
2. "What Is a Standard Drink?"
3. "What Is a Standard Drink?"
4. "What Is a Standard Drink?"
5. "Alcohol Fermentation." *CK-12*. CK-12 Foundation, n.d. Web. 20 Feb. 2018.
6. Frank M. Shipman and Alan T. Thomas. "Distilled Spirit." *Encyclopedia Britannica*. Encyclopedia Britannica, n.d. Web. 20 Feb. 2018.

CHAPTER 3. ALCOHOL AND CULTURE

1. Jayesh B. Shah. "The History of Wound Care." *Journal of the American College of Clinical Wound Specialists* 3.3 (2012): 65–66. Print.
2. Mark E. Rose. *Alcohol: Its History, Pharmacology, and Treatment*. Center City, MN: Hazelden, 2011. Print. 13.
3. "Unintended Consequences." *PBS.org*. WETA, n.d. Web. 20 Feb. 2018.
4. "Unintended Consequences."
5. Jennifer Latson. "A Toast to the End of Prohibition." *Time*. Time, 5 Dec. 2014. Web. 20 Feb. 2018.
6. Latson, "A Toast to the End of Prohibition."
7. Jean Kinney. *Loosening the Grip: A Handbook of Alcohol Information*. New York: McGraw-Hill, 2015. Print. 35.
8. Robin A. LaVallee, et al. "Apparent Per Capita Alcohol Consumption: National, State, and Regional Trends, 1977–2012." *National Institute on Alcohol Abuse and Alcoholism*. US Department of Health & Human Services, Apr. 2014. Web. 20 Feb. 2018.

CHAPTER 4. EFFECTS ON THE BRAIN AND BODY

1. Mark Keller and George E. Vaillant. "Alcohol Consumption." *Encyclopedia Britannica*. Encyclopedia Britannica, n.d. Web. 20 Feb. 2018.

2. Akikur Mohammad. *The Anatomy of Addiction*. New York: Perigee, 2016. Print. 72.

3. Cynthia Kuhn. *Just Say Know: Talking with Kids about Drugs and Alcohol*. New York: Norton, 2002. Print. 61–62.

4. Kuhn, *Just Say Know: Talking with Kids about Drugs and Alcohol*, 63.

5. "DUI & DWI." *DMV.org*. DMV.org, n.d. Web. 20 Feb. 2018.

6. Keller and Vaillant, "Alcohol Consumption."

7. "What Is a Blood Alcohol Test?" *WebMD*. WebMD, n.d. Web. 20 Feb. 2018.

8. Mark E. Rose. *Alcohol: Its History, Pharmacology, and Treatment*. Center City, MN: Hazelden, 2011. Print. 78.

9. "Alcohol Poisoning Deaths." *Centers for Disease Control and Prevention*. US Department of Health & Human Services, Jan. 2015. Web. 20 Feb. 2018.

CHAPTER 5. LONG-TERM EFFECTS OF ALCOHOL USE

1. "F. Scott Fitzgerald." *Baltimore Literary Heritage Project*. University of Baltimore, n.d. Web. 20 Feb. 2018.

2. Mark E. Rose. *Alcohol: Its History, Pharmacology, and Treatment*. Center City, MN: Hazelden, 2011. Print. 1.

3. Rose, *Alcohol: Its History, Pharmacology, and Treatment*, 1.

4. "Alcohol Facts and Statistics." *National Institute on Alcohol Abuse and Alcoholism*. US Department of Health & Human Services, June 2017. Web. 20 Feb. 2018.

CHAPTER 6. YOUNG ADULT ALCOHOL USE

1. "Fact Sheets—Underage Drinking." *Centers for Disease Control and Prevention*. US Department of Health & Human Services, n.d. Web. 20 Feb. 2018.

2. "Alcohol Facts and Statistics." *National Institute on Alcohol Abuse and Alcoholism*. US Department of Health & Human Services, June 2017. Web. 20 Feb. 2018.

3. "Underage Drinking: A Major Public Health Challenge." *National Institute on Alcohol Abuse and Alcoholism*. US Department of Health & Human Services, June 2003. Web. 20 Feb. 2018.

4. Katy Butler. "The Grim Neurology of Teenage Drinking." *New York Times*. New York Times Company, 4 July 2006. Web. 20 Feb. 2018.

5. "Fact Sheets—Underage Drinking."

6. "Drinking Levels Defined." *National Institute on Alcohol Abuse and Alcoholism*. US Department of Health & Human Services, n.d. Web. 20 Feb. 2018.

7. "Fact Sheets—Underage Drinking."

8. Cynthia Kuhn. *Just Say Know: Talking with Kids about Drugs and Alcohol*. New York: Norton, 2002. Print. 67.

SOURCE NOTES CONTINUED

CHAPTER 7. SOCIAL COSTS

1. "The Problem." *MADD*. MADD, n.d. Web. 20 Feb. 2018.
2. Mark E. Rose. *Alcohol: Its History, Pharmacology, and Treatment*. Center City, MN: Hazelden, 2011. Print. 71.
3. "The Problem."
4. "Sober to Start." *MADD*. MADD, n.d. Web. 20 Feb. 2018.
5. "Drunk Driving Prevention." *Ad Council*. Ad Council, n.d. Web. 20 Feb. 2018.
6. "Our Story." *MADD*. MADD, n.d. Web. 20 Feb. 2018.
7. "Motorcycles." *Insurance Institute for Highway Safety, Highway Loss Data Institute*. Insurance Institute for Highway Safety, Highway Loss Data Institute, Dec. 2017. Web. 20 Feb. 2018.
8. Rose, *Alcohol: Its History, Pharmacology, and Treatment*, 85.
9. "Alcohol, Drugs and Crime." *National Council on Alcoholism and Drug Dependence*. NCADD, n.d. Web. 20 Feb. 2018.
10. "Dangerous Liaisons: Substance Abuse and Sex." *National Center on Addiction and Substance Abuse*. National Center on Addiction and Substance Abuse, Dec. 1999. Web. 20 Feb. 2018.
11. "Alcohol Facts and Statistics." *National Institute on Alcohol Abuse and Alcoholism*. US Department of Health & Human Services, June 2017. Web. 20 Feb. 2018.
12. Rose, *Alcohol: Its History, Pharmacology, and Treatment*, 67.
13. "Fetal Alcohol Syndrome (FAS)." *Centers for Disease Control and Prevention*. US Department of Health & Human Services, 15 Sept. 2017. Web. 20 Feb. 2018.

CHAPTER 8. LAWS AND POLICIES

1. "Global Status Report on Alcohol and Health 2014." *World Health Organization*. WHO, 2014. Web. 20 Feb. 2018.
2. "The National Minimum Drinking Age Act of 1984." *Legal Flip*. ThinkingLegal, n.d. Web. 20 Feb. 2018.
3. "What Caused the Decrease?" *National Highway Traffic Safety Administration*. US Department of Transportation, n.d. Web. 20 Feb. 2018.
4. Jean Kinney. *Loosening the Grip: A Handbook of Alcohol Information*. New York: McGraw-Hill, 2015. Print. 19.
5. Kinney, *Loosening the Grip*, 25.
6. "Alcohol Advertising." *Federal Trade Commission*. Federal Trade Commission, n.d. Web. 20 Feb. 2018.
7. "Alcohol Advertising and Youth." *Johns Hopkins Bloomberg School of Public Health*. Johns Hopkins University, n.d. Web. 20 Feb. 2018.

CHAPTER 9. RECOVERING FROM ALCOHOL USE DISORDER

1. Richard Taite. "Can Alcoholics Ever Drink Moderately?" *Psychology Today*. Sussex Publishers, 8 Apr. 2014. Web. 20 Feb. 2018.

2. "Definition of Recovery." *National Council on Alcoholism and Drug Dependence*. NCADD, n.d. Web. 20 Feb. 2018.

3. "A.A.'s Big Book, Alcoholics Anonymous, and Twelve Steps and Twelve Traditions Now Available in eBook Format." *Alcoholics Anonymous*. Alcoholics Anonymous World Services, 12 Jan. 2012. Web. 20 Feb. 2018.

4. Mark E. Rose. *Alcohol: Its History, Pharmacology, and Treatment*. Center City, MN: Hazelden, 2011. Print. 149.

INDEX

ABOUT THE AUTHOR

Lisa J. Amstutz is the author of many children's books and articles. She specializes in topics related to science, nature, and agriculture. Her background includes a BA in biology and an MS in environmental science/ecology. When Lisa isn't writing, you may find her tramping through the woods or curled up with a cup of tea and a good book.